Read *the* Bible *for* One Hour Every Day *for* 92 Days

David Eli Hittle

WESTBOW
PRESS®
A DIVISION OF THOMAS NELSON
& ZONDERVAN

WestBow Press books may be ordered through booksellers or by contacting:

WestBow Press
A Division of Thomas Nelson & Zondervan
1663 Liberty Drive
Bloomington, IN 47403
www.westbowpress.com
1 (866) 928-1240

ISBN: 978-1-9736-9200-3 (sc)
ISBN: 978-1-9736-9202-7 (hc)
ISBN: 978-1-9736-9201-0 (e)

Library of Congress Control Number: 2020909074

Print information available on the last page.

WestBow Press rev. date: 5/19/2020

INTRODUCTION

>-+◆>-O-<◆+-<

When I first decided to read the Bible from Genesis to Revelation, it seemed to be almost impossible. My first attempt started with the King James Version. I retained very little of what I read. My second reading was the Living Bible, and I retained more and got more of an overview of what the Bible was saying. I was then able to read the King James Version with a better understanding. I decided to read another version, and when I would read something that sounded strange or odd, I compared it with King James. I then decided to read as many versions as I could get my hands on.

One year I read the *One New Man Bible*. Ephesians 2:15 says that God took the Jews and Gentiles and joined the two to create, "one new man" (with Christ being the cornerstone). This translation listed the Old Testament books in the traditional Jewish order. I think it's much easier to read in that order because of the smooth transition from the Old to the New Testament. Now when I read any version, this is the order I use: Genesis, Exodus, Leviticus, Numbers, Deuteronomy, Joshua, Judges, 1 Samuel, 2 Samuel, 1 Kings, 2 Kings, Isaiah, Jeremiah, Ezekiel, Hosea, Joel, Amos, Obadiah, Jonah, Micah, Nahum, Habakkuk, Zephaniah, Haggai, Zechariah, Malachi, Psalms, Proverbs, Job, Song of Songs, Ruth, Lamentations, Ecclesiastes, Esther, Daniel, Ezra, Nehemiah, 1 Chronicles, 2 Chronicles (then Matthew). The New Testament sequence is the Christian book order.

This is not a speed-reading contest, so I have tried to break it into one-hour readings. The key is to set aside an hour each day for reading. It is best to read at the same time every day so it becomes habit. I like to read in the morning, before anyone else is up so there is little or no distraction. You may have to adjust your bedtime for this. Maybe you could skip watching the news. Or maybe you could give up two sitcoms. You decide. God's blessings as you read. Some people find it helpful to read this book first to get an overview. Others find it helpful to break each days reading in half, reading half an hour each day. Let's get started!

DAY 1

>━┥◆❯━O━❮◆┝━<

Genesis 1 to Genesis 18

God creates the heavens and the earth and put Adam and Eve in the garden. Cain kills Abel. God tells Noah to build an ark. After the flood, God sets the rainbow as a sign to all generations. God confuses the people's language so they will be scattered and populate the earth. God changes Abram's name to Abraham. The account of creation until the covenant of circumcision is about 2,045 years. (Abraham was ninety-nine years old.)

DAY 2

Genesis 18 to Genesis 28

Abraham is one hundred years old, Ishmael is fourteen, and Sarah is ninety when Isaac is born. Sarah lives to be 127 years old. Abraham lives to be 175 years old. Isaac is forty when he marries Rebekah, and sixty when the twins (Jacob and Esau) are born.

DAY 3

Genesis 28 to Genesis 38

Jacob works for Laban for twenty years. As he returns to Canaan, God changes his name to Israel. Isaac lives to be 180 years old. Esau moves to Seir. Joseph has two dreams when he is seventeen, so his brothers sell him as a slave.

DAY 4

Genesis 38 to Genesis 49

In Egypt, Joseph is sent to prison for a crime he didn't commit. When he is thirty years old, he is made ruler over Egypt under Pharaoh. Jacob (Israel) is 130 years old when he moves his family to Egypt and dies when he is 147 years old.

DAY 5

Genesis 49 to Exodus 12

All the plagues of Egypt occur, and Pharaoh's heart is still hardened against God's people. One more plague remains.

DAY 6

>━╾╼━◦━╾╼━<

Exodus 12 to Exodus 21

The final plague: all the firstborn children of Egypt die at midnight on the same night. Passover is established because God passed over the Israelites, and not one of them died. So after living in Egypt for 430 years, Israel escapes through the Red Sea (Sea of Reeds). God gives them manna (bread) from heaven to eat for forty years. The Ten Commandments are given.

DAY 7

Exodus 21 to Exodus 32

God gives the Law (Torah) and then calls Moses to the top of the mountain. He stays there for forty days and forty nights and receives the tablets and instructions for the tabernacle, its furnishings, the priests, the consecration, and so on.

DAY 8

Exodus 32 to Leviticus 4

Aaron makes the golden calf! Moses breaks the tablets and returns to the mountain for another forty days and forty nights. The tabernacle is completed and set up on the first day of their second year.

DAY 9

Leviticus 4 to Leviticus 14

The priest makes atonement for himself and the people. The ordination of Aaron and his sons takes seven days. Nadab and Abihu die. God gives regulations for food that may or may not be eaten.

DAY 10

Leviticus 14 to Leviticus 23

The priest pronounces a person clean or unclean. The Day of Atonement is once a year. Blood must not be eaten because the life is in the blood. God's laws set you apart from the nations. Be holy because God is holy.

DAY 11

Leviticus 23 to Numbers 3

Instructions for the feasts of the Lord and the year of Jubilee. You can follow the decrees of God and be blessed, or if not, be cursed. In Numbers, the army is counted and numbered. (Why do they call it Numbers?)

DAY 12

Numbers 3 to Numbers 11

The Levite males one month old or more are counted. Then all the firstborn Israelite males are counted. The Nazirite vow is established. The dedication of the Altar takes twelve days, one day for each tribe: Judah, Issachar, Zebulun, Ruben, Simeon, Gad, Ephraim, Manasseh, Benjamin, Dan, Asher, and Naphtali. The Levites are to serve Aaron and his sons. A cloud by day and the fire by night are over the tabernacle. The two silver trumpets are for signaling the community.

DAY 13

Numbers 11 to Numbers 21

The people complain about the food, so God sends quail. Miriam and Aaron also complain about Moses. The twelve spies are sent into Canaan and return with some of the fruit. The Israelites return to the desert for forty years. Because of rebellion in the Levite tribe, the earth swallows them alive. Aaron's staff produces almonds. Miriam dies at Kadesh, and Aaron dies at Mount Hor.

DAY 14

Numbers 21 to Numbers 31

God tells Moses to make a bronze snake and puts it on a pole. The king of Moab sends for Balaam to curse Israel. But he can only bless them, so the women of Moab seduce the men of Israel. Moses counts the men who can serve in the army; the Levites do not serve in the army. Moses reminds the community about the offerings to be made by fire.

DAY 15

><+>+O+<+><

Numbers 31 to Deuteronomy 4

Moses is told he will be gathered to his people after he takes vengeance on Midian. Balaam is killed in the battle. Not one of the Israelites are killed in battle, and the land is allotted to the tribes of Gad, Ruben, and the half tribe of Manasseh. The land across the Jordan River will be divided by casting lots. The Levites will be given towns, pastureland, and cities of refuge. No inheritance may pass from tribe to tribe. Moses then reminds the community about their journey from Egypt. Joshua is commissioned to lead the people after Moses departs.

DAY 16

Deuteronomy 4 to Deuteronomy 13

Moses reminds the community how everyone twenty years old or older died in the desert; only Joshua and Caleb were still living. Three cities east of the Jordan River are set aside as cities of refuge. "Remember the Law (Torah) given at Mount Horeb and teach it to your children. God will send bees (hornets) to help drive the enemy out. Abhor, detest, and destroy the idols; do not put them in your house."

DAY 17

>━┼╺◆╸━◯━╺◆╸┼━<

Deuteronomy 13 to Deuteronomy 26

Moses continues to recite the Law (Torah) before the community. "Purge the false prophets from among you. Eat no unclean animals, pay the tithe, and cancel all debts every seven years. All firstborn male animals belong to God. All the men are to stand before the Lord three times a year. Never move a boundary stone. Never leave a dead man hanging on a tree overnight. Pay a hired man his wages every day. Completely destroy the Amalekites."

DAY 18

>─┤◆>─●─<◆┤─<

Deuteronomy 26 to the end of Deuteronomy

"Build an altar on Mount Ebal, coat it with plaster, and write the Law (Torah) on it. Proclaim blessings from Mount Gerizim and curses from Mount Ebal — blessings if you obey, curses if you disobey. Remember that in the forty years spent in the desert, your clothes and shoes never wore out." Moses gives them a song as a witness against them. Moses blesses the tribes and then climbs Mount Nebo, where he sees all of the Promised Land. Moses is 120 years old, and neither his eyes nor his strength are gone.

DAY 19

>━┼━◆>━◦━◇┼━◁

Joshua 1 to Joshua 12

Joshua sends two spies to Jericho. Rahab helps the spies and saves her family. The Israelites cross the Jordan and observe Passover on the fourteenth day of the first month, then manna stops. Jericho is defeated, but Achan takes some of the devoted things. Ai is defeated, so Gibeon deceives Israel into making a peace treaty. The sun stops in the middle of the sky while Israel defeats the Amorites. Joshua takes the whole land, and the land has rest from war.

DAY 20

Joshua 12 to Joshua 22

Listed are the kings east of the Jordan taken by Moses and west of the Jordan taken by Joshua. The land is divided by casting lots at Shiloh, where the "Tent of Meeting" was set up. Caleb is eighty-five years old when the land is divided, and he drives out the three sons of Anak the giant. The five daughters of Zelophehad are given an inheritance. The cities of refuge are named. The forty-eight Levite towns with pasturelands are also named.

DAY 21

Joshua 22 to Judges 9

Reuben, Gad, and Manasseh return east of the Jordan and build an altar. Joshua renews the covenant and lives to be 110 years old. Joseph's bones are buried at Shechem. Israel starts worshipping false gods, so God appoints judges. Heber the Kenite (Moses' brother-in-law) has a wife named Jael who kills Sisera, commander of the Canaanite army. Gideon defeats the Midianite army. Gideon has many wives and seventy sons. He also has a son by another woman and named him Abimelech.

DAY 22

Judges 9 to Judges 19.

Abimelech, son of Jerubbaal (Gideon), kills his seventy half-brothers, except for Jotham, the youngest. Shechem crowns Abimelech king. Abimelech is killed when a woman drops a millstone on his head. Jephthah the Gileadite, the son of a prostitute, is driven away by his half-brothers. He becomes a warrior and defeats the Ammonites but loses his daughter. Samson, a Danite, tells Delilah his secret about his strength, and the Philistines put out his eyes. The Danites capture Laish and rename it Dan.

DAY 23

Judges 19 to 1 Samuel 9 (skip Ruth)

A Levite from Ephraim goes to Bethlehem in Judah to get his wife, who had returned to her father's house. They spend the night in Gibeah (in Benjamin). The men of the city kill his wife, so all Israel fights with Benjamin and kill all but six hundred men. Israel comes up with a plan so the six hundred Benjamites can each have a wife. Samuel goes to live with Eli the priest. The Philistines capture the ark of the Lords covenant but keep it only seven months. Israel tells Samuel they want a king like the other nations.
(Note: You have read one quarter of the Bible.)

DAY 24

1 Samuel 9 to 1 Samuel 18

Samuel anoints Saul king when he is thirty years old. He reigns for forty-two years. Saul's first cousin, Abner, is commander of the army. Saul is told to destroy the Amalekites, which he does not do. Samuel anoints David king. David, a young boy, kills Goliath with a sling and stone. (Saul reigns for twelve years before David is born. David is thirty years old when crowned.)

DAY 25

1 Samuel 18 to the end of 1 Samuel

Saul is jealous of David and tries to kill him. David marries Michal, Saul's daughter. Saul orders David's death, but he escapes with the help of Michal, Jonathan, and the priest of Nob. Saul kills the priests and people of Nob. One of the priests, Abiathar, escapes and joins David and his six hundred men. David spares Saul's life twice. Saul gives Michal to another man. David has two wives, Ahinoam and Abigail. Ziklag is destroyed by the Amalekites. (See days 17 and 24.) David recovers everything. Saul and Jonathan are killed in battle. An Amalekite gives Saul the final deadly blow.

DAY 26

2 Samuel 1 to 2 Samuel 13

David is anointed king in Hebron over the tribe of Judah when he is thirty years old. Abner, Saul's cousin, anoints Saul's son Ish-Bosheth king over Israel. Joab, Asahel, and Abishai (David's sisters' sons) meet Abner, and the war starts. Abner kills Asahel, and Joab kills Abner. Two men kill Ish-Bosheth and take his head to David. David kills the two men and mourns for Abner. David becomes king over all Israel. David sleeps with Bathsheba and then has her husband killed to cover the sin because she becomes pregnant. The child dies, and Bathsheba has another son and names him Solomon. David is told the sword will never depart from his house.

DAY 27

2 Samuel 13 to 2 Samuel 22

Trouble starts for David's house. His son Amnon rapes his half-sister Tamar. Her brother, Absalom, kills Amnon and flees from Jerusalem. He is gone for three years before he is allowed to return. David will not see him for another two years. Absalom sets himself up as king, so David leaves the palace. Absalom rapes the ten women David left behind to attend the palace. Absalom is killed in battle when his hair gets caught in a tree. David returns to Jerusalem as king.

DAY 28

2 Samuel 22 to 1 Kings 7

Chapter 22 is a song (psalm) of David to the Lord. David's mighty men are listed, and the chapter tells why they are called mighty. Some are like a one-man army. Among David's mighty men are Uriah, Bathsheba's husband. David counts the fighting men, and God sends a plague. David builds an altar on the threshing floor. A virgin, Abishag, is to keep David warm. Adonijah sets himself up as king. David tells Zadok and Nathan to anoint Solomon king. Solomon kills Adonijah, Joab, and Shimei. Solomon asks for wisdom. Hiram, king of Tyre, makes a deal with Solomon. Four years after becoming king, Solomon starts building the temple, which takes seven years to complete. The inside of the temple is overlaid with gold.

DAY 29

1 Kings 7 to 1 Kings 14

Solomon takes thirteen years to build his palace. They use clay molds to cast the bronze pillars, the capitals, the sea, the bulls, and so on. Other items are made of pure gold. When the ark of the Lords covenant is brought in, the glory cloud fills the temple. Solomon prays and then blesses the people. God again appears to Solomon. Hiram, the king of Tyre, is displeased with the towns Solomon gave him. The queen of Sheba visits Jerusalem. Solomon makes two hundred large shields and three hundred small shields from pure gold. Solomon has seven hundred wives and three hundred concubines, which lead him to his downfall (sin). Jeroboam, son of Nebat, is told he will be king over ten tribes. Solomon dies, and the new king, his son REHOBOAM, is harsh with the people, so the kingdom is split. Only Judah and Benjamin remain loyal to REHOBOAM. Jeroboam sets up the golden calves and makes priests from common people. A prophet from Judah rebukes Jeroboam and is killed by a lion when he disobeys God.

Special Note: From here on, it is difficult to keep the kings of the northern kingdom (Israel) separate (in your head) from the kings of Judah (the southern kingdom) so the kings of Judah will be capitalized letters. Both kingdoms fall into sin, but Judah is more loyal than the northern kingdom, from now on called Israel.

DAY 30

>━┼━◆>━◆━O━◆>━┼━≺

1 Kings 14 to the end of 1 Kings

Jeroboam is told his whole family will be destroyed. He reigns for twenty-two years. REHOBOAM was forty-one years old when he becomes king in Jerusalem and reigns seventeen years. The king of Egypt plunders the palace and the temple, and takes all the gold shields Solomon had made. REHOBOAM replaces the shields with bronze. His son ABIJAH is the next king of Judah and reigns three years. His son ASA is the next king, and he reigns for forty-one years. His son JEHOSHAPHAT is the next king of Judah. Nadab, son of Jeroboam, becomes king of Israel and reigns two years. Baasha kills Nadab and his family and becomes king for twenty-four years. Elah, the next king in Israel, reigns two years. Zimri kills Elah and his family and reigns seven days. Zimri burns to death. Omri becomes king and builds Samaria. Omri reigns twelve years, and his son Ahab becomes king in Samaria and reigns twenty-two years. Ahab marries Jezebel. Elijah the prophet tells Ahab there will be no rain. Elijah goes to a widow in Zarephath who supplies him with food from God for three years. Elijah returns to Ahab, and they meet at Mt. Carmel with the 450 prophets of Baal. Elijah hides from Jezebel. God tells Elijah to anoint Jehu king of Israel and anoint Elisha to succeed him (Elijah) as prophet. The king of Aram is defeated by Ahab with God's help, but Ahab lets him go. Jezebel kills Naboth. JEHOSHAPHAT teams up with Ahab to fight with the king of Aram, and Ahab is killed. Ahaziah, Ahab's son, reigns for two years.

DAY 31

>–·‹◆›·•O•·‹◆›·–‹

2 Kings 1 to 2 Kings 11

Ahaziah dies with no sons, so Jehoram reigns for twelve years. Elijah is taken to heaven while Elisha watches. JEHOSHAPHAT teams up with Jehoram, king of Israel, this time against Moab. A widow and her two sons get enough oil to pay her debt. A Shunammite woman's son is raised from the dead. Naaman is healed of leprosy, and Gehazi gets leprosy. The king of Aram goes to war with Israel, and there is a great famine in Samaria. JEHOSHAPHAT dies, and his son JEHORAM is king of Judah for eight years. His son AHAZIAH reigns for a year in Jerusalem. Jehu is again anointed king of Israel, and he kills the king of Israel and the king of Judah. Jezebel is tossed out of a window. Jehu kills all of Ahab's family, chief men, priests of Baal, his friends, and prophets of Baal. God begins to reduce the size of Israel. Jehu reigns in Samaria for twenty-eight years, and then his son Jehoahaz becomes king.

DAY 32

>─┤─◆>─●─<◆>─┤─<

2 Kings 11 to 2 Kings 18

ATHALIAH, mother of AHAZIAH, hears of her son's death, kills the royal family, and takes the throne. Joash, AHAZIAH's youngest son, is hidden by his aunt. When JOASH is seven years old, Jehoiada, the priest proclaims him king in Jerusalem, and he reigns forty years. ATHALIAH is put to death. JOASH is assassinated, and his son AMAZIAH is king for twenty-nine years. In Samaria, Jehoahaz, Jehu's son, is king for seventeen years. His son Jeroboam is king in Samaria for forty-one years. AMAZIAH, king of Judah, is murdered, and his son UZZIAH is king for fifty-two years. Jeroboam (king of Israel) dies, and his son Zechariah reigns for six months. JOTHAM, son of UZZIAH, is king for sixteen years. In Samaria, Shallum kills Zechariah in front of the people and is king for one month. Menahem kills Shallum and takes the kingship for ten years. Menahem's son Pekahiah is king for two years and is assassinated by Pekah, who reigns for twenty years. Assyria begins deporting the people of Israel. Hoshea, Israel's last king, kills Pekah and reigns nine years. Assyria captures Samaria. AHAZ, son of JOTHAM, is king in Jerusalem for sixteen years. He builds an altar like the one in Damascus. HEZEKIAH succeeds AHAZ as king and reigns twenty-nine years.

DAY 33

>—‹◆›—O—‹◆›—‹

2 Kings 18 to the end of 2 Kings; Isaiah chapter 1

HEZEKIAH smashes the bronze snake made by Moses in the desert. The king of Assyria captures the walled cities of Judah. HEZEKIAH strips the gold off the temple doors and doorposts. The king of Assyria tells Jerusalem that God cannot deliver them, so God sends an angel to kill 185,000 Assyrian men. The king of Babylon sends HEZEKIAH a gift. MANASSEH, son of HEZEKIAH, is king in Jerusalem for fifty-five years. MANASSEH fills Jerusalem with innocent blood. His son AMON is king for two years and is assassinated; his son JOSIAH is king for thirty-one years. The high priest finds the Book of the Law (Torah). JOSIAH celebrates the Passover. The king of Egypt kills JOSIAH and his son; JEHOAHAZ is made king in Jerusalem for three months. The king of Egypt removes him, sets ELIAKIM as king, and changes his name to JEHOIAKIM. He reigns eleven years. His son JEHOIACHIN is king for three months. The king of Babylon captures Jerusalem and puts MATTANIAH in charge, changing his name to ZEDEKIAH. He reigns eleven years. The walls of Jerusalem are broken down; the temple, the palace, and houses are burned. GEDALIAH is left in charge and is assassinated after seven months. The people flee to Egypt.

In the book of Isaiah, Isaiah the prophet ministers under UZZIAH, JOTHAM, AHAZ, and HEZEKIAH in Jerusalem.

DAY 34

Isaiah 2 to Isaiah 15

In the last days, the mountain of the Lord's house is established. Nations no longer go to war, and the Lord is exalted. The righteous enjoy life, but woe to the wicked. The bloodstains of Jerusalem are cleansed. The vineyard of the Lord is Israel, his garden, Judah. "Woe to those who call evil good, and good evil." Isaiah sees the Lord on the throne and the seraphim with six wings. "Do not fear man, but fear God. Do not consult the dead for the living. The light shines on those who walk in darkness (sin), for unto us a child is born (Jesus). A branch—Jesus—will grow from the root of Jesse, and the earth is full of the knowledge of the Lord. The morning star, Satan, is cast down to the earth. Assyria's yoke is broken, and the Philistines are destroyed by famine."

DAY 35

>━┤◆>━O━<◆┤━<

Isaiah 15 to Isaiah 32

Moab will be ruined in a single night; water is dried up, and joy and gladness are removed. Within three years, the people are despised. Damascus (in Syria) will be in ruins and turn to God. In Egypt, the Nile will dry up. Judah will bring terror to the Egyptians, and then they will worship God. A highway will go from Egypt to Assyria. Babylon will fall. Jerusalem is full of tumult because they did not look to God. Tyre is destroyed for seventy years. The Lord will distort the face of the earth; it will "shake violently and reel to and fro." God is a stronghold for the poor, and death will be swallowed up. Although favor (grace) is shown to the wicked, they go on doing evil. Israel will fill the earth with fruit, and a great trumpet will sound. The Lord will be a crown for the remnant, a cornerstone in Zion (Jerusalem). The farmer's wisdom comes from God. The vision is sealed until the end, and the house of Jacob—Israel and Judah—will not be ashamed. The Lord longs to show mercy. He will defend Jerusalem.

DAY 36

Isaiah 32 to Isaiah 44

The "King of Righteousness" is coming. There will be peace, quietness, and confidence in your resting place. The Lord is exalted. The key is to fear the Lord. Who can walk like this? The righteous! The Lord is our judge. "The heavens will be rolled up like a scroll; the desert will blossom and rejoice. There will be a highway of holiness." The king of Assyria mocks HEZEKIAH and God, so God puts a "hook in his nose," and his two sons assassinate him. HEZEKIAH is told he will die, but God adds fifteen years to his life. The king of Babylon hears about his recovery and sees all the gold and silver in the palace and temple. A voice cries in the wilderness, "prepare the way of the Lord," God sits on the circle of the earth; he is strong in power. Wait on the Lord and renew your strength. God will place pools of water in the desert, establish justice in the earth, and guide the blind. God calls his people from the East, West, North, and South. Behold, he will do a new thing.

DAY 37

>━┤━◆>━O━<◆>━┤━<

Isaiah 44 to Isaiah 55

"God will pour out his spirit, but those who worship idols cannot see or understand. There is no other God but the Lord. Let salvation and righteousness spring up together. Every knee will bow before God, and he will take vengeance on Babylon. The stargazers and prognosticators (false prophets) cannot help you. God has foretold the future, so you cannot say your idol has done anything. If only you had followed the commandments, you would have peace like a river. For the wicked, there is no peace. All flesh will know I am the God of Jacob. The heavens will vanish like smoke, and the earth will wear out! The redeemed will come singing to Zion, Jerusalem. The cup of the Lord's fury will be handed to your enemy. Break into singing and joy. The whole earth will see the salvation of God. We have all gone astray (like sheep), but he—the Lamb of God, Jesus—has taken all our iniquity and become our sin offering (Passover lamb)."

DAY 38

><+>•O•<+><

Isaiah 55 to the end of Isaiah

Don't wait to seek the Lord; he will not always be near. Do not be wicked and change your thoughts, so God can show his mercy. Then the trees of the field will clap their hands. God accepts the foreigner as well as the eunuch, and his house will be called a house of prayer for all people. "You mock me and stick out your tongue when you worship idols. Can they save you when you cry out to them? They cannot give you rest or peace! Raise your voice like a trumpet and declare their rebellion. They fast, but not to me, and they end in fighting." (Seek God and he will lift you up.) No one wants justice. You run to evil and grope like the blind. Darkness covers the earth, but God's glory will be seen even by the Gentiles. Foreigners will rebuild your walls because of God's mercy. God will be your everlasting light. You will be called "Priests of the Lord," and the Gentiles will see your righteousness. You will be the Lord's delight. They will call you "the holy people, the redeemed of the Lord." God had vengeance in his heart, but now redemption. Remember the days of Moses. You cannot perceive what God has in store for those who seek him. We are clay; God is the potter. He extends his hands to the rebellious. He creates a new heaven and new earth. Even the wild animals will eat alongside the domestic animals. God has regard for the humble who fear his word. The Lord's chariots are like the whirlwind and fire with the sword, and all humankind will "bow before him."

DAY 39

>─┤◆╳─O─╳◆┤─<

Jeremiah 1 to Jeremiah 14

Jeremiah is from Anathoth, a city of the priests, in Benjamin (of Judah). He ministered in Jerusalem under the kings JOSIAH, JEHOAHAZ, JEHOIAKIM, JEHOIACHIN, ZEDEKIAH, and GEDALIAH. God called him before he was born. God speaks against the wickedness of the people and promises Jeremiah his protection. The people no longer fear God and think it's okay to worship idols. They think they are innocent. The people of Judah saw how God dealt with Israel (the northern kingdom) and are still unrepentant. "Blow the trumpet in Judah, wash the evil from your heart. You are wise in doing evil, but foolish in knowledge. Turn back to God, or your land will become desolate. Study the old path, the good way. Your idol worship provokes me to anger. I warned your forefathers but they were stiff-necked, even sacrificing the children in the fire. Everyone asks, "What have I done wrong?" They say peace, peace, but there is no peace. Therefore I will send snakes (vipers) to bite you and I will scatter you among the nations. You are cursed because you did not follow the covenant." Jeremiah is told to get a linen belt and bury it. After many days, he is told to dig it up. It was ruined. Totally worthless, just like Jerusalem and Judah will be. God will scatter you, and your shame will be exposed.

DAY 40

>───┤◆├──○──┤◆├──┤─<

Jeremiah 14 to Jeremiah 26

Jeremiah is told the prophets are false. Moses and Samuel cannot plead for them because of what MANNESSAH did. The false prophets will fight against Jeremiah but not prevail. Jeremiah is forbidden to have a wife because of what will happen in Jerusalem. The heart is deceitful, and God searches everyone. Jeremiah watches as the potter remakes a marred pot. He then buys a clay jar and smashes it before the elders and priests, comparing it to Jerusalem. The chief officer (priest) has him beaten and put in the stocks. ZEDEKIAH, the king, sends for Jeremiah because Nebuchadnezzar declares war. Jeremiah tells them if they surrender, they will live; but if not, they will die in the city. "Woe to the shepherds (false prophets) who destroy my sheep. I (God) will raise up a righteous branch (Jesus) from the line of David. The false prophets spread wickedness across the land." Jeremiah has a vision of good figs—the exiles—and bad figs—Judah's officials.

DAY 41

Jeremiah 26 to Jeremiah 34

Jeremiah is told to stand in the courtyard and say everything God tells him. The officials said, "This man must die." Some of the elders spare Jeremiah's life. Jeremiah puts a wooden yoke on his own neck as a sign they will be in bondage to Babylon. The false prophet Hananiah says that in two years, the exiles will return. He then breaks the wooden yoke on Jeremiah's neck. Jeremiah tells Hananiah that he will die within a year. Two months later, he dies. Jeremiah writes a letter to the exiles in Babylon and tells them they will be there seventy years. Shemaiah, an official, calls Jeremiah a madman. God tells Jeremiah to write a book to encourage the exiles. "There is hope, I (God) will make a new covenant with Israel and Judah." The king of Babylon besieges Jerusalem, and ZEDEKIAH imprisons Jeremiah in the courtyard. Jeremiah buys a field and then asks God, "Why did you tell me to buy a field?"

DAY 42

>‑I‑‹›‑‑O‑‑‹›‑I‑‹

Jeremiah 34 to Jeremiah 46

ZEDEKIAH is told he will see the king of Babylon face-to-face. ZEDEKIAH sets the slaves free, but some of the people enslave them again. Jeremiah sets the Recabite family as a good example of faithfulness. Jeremiah writes a scroll, and ZEDEKIAH burns it up, so he rewrites it. The officials want Jeremiah put to death, so they put him in a cistern. ZEDEKIAH calls Jeremiah again and then locks him in the courtyard. ZEDEKIAH is captured, and his sons are killed before his eyes. Then his eyes are put out. Nebuchadnezzar sets Jeremiah free. GEDALIAH is assassinated, and the people flee to Egypt, though they are warned not to return to Egypt. The people are stubborn and continue to worship the "Queen of Heaven."

DAY 43

>━┼━◆>━❖━<◆>━┼━<

Jeremiah 46 to the end of Jeremiah

A section of warnings. Against Egypt, they are told they will be handed over to Nebuchadnezzar. Against the Philistines, they are told, the Lord will destroy them. Against Moab, descendants of Lot, they are told, the sword will pursue you who say, "We are valiant warriors in battle." You have defied the Lord. Against Ammon, descendants of Lot, they are told, terror from those around you, and you will be driven away. Against Edom, Esau, You will be an object of horror, like Sodom and Gomorrah. Against Damascus, Syria, Your young men will fall in the streets in one day. Against Kedar and Hazor, Ishmaelites, they are told to hide in the caves. Babylon has plotted against you. Against Babylon, You will be captured from the north. You will be like Sodom and Gomorrah because of what you have done in Zion (Jerusalem). Your walls will be leveled and your gates burned.

DAY 44

>─┤─◆─○─◆─┤─<

Ezekiel 1 to Ezekiel 15
(skip Lamentations)

The priest Ezekiel is exiled to Babylon. In a vision he sees a windstorm surrounded by brilliant light with four creatures inside the cloud of fire. Each creature has four faces: a man, a lion, an ox, and an eagle. Above it is a throne with a figure like a man seated. It was the glory of the Lord. A voice speaks and sends him to the Israelites as a prophet and gives him a scroll to eat. Seven days later, he is told what to do: Lie on his left side for 390 days, and then on his right side for 40 days. Shave his head and beard and divide it into three parts. (The three parts stand for three judgments: the sword, famine, and scattering the remnant). Those who escape will be covered with terror. Their gold and silver idols will be worthless. In another vision, Ezekiel is taken to Jerusalem, where the elders are worshipping idols and filling the land with violence. A man dressed in linen marks those who fear God, and the rest are slain. The man in linen gets burning coals to scatter over Jerusalem. Ezekiel sees the leaders who plot evil and give wicked advice. God promises to return the remnant who were scattered to the nations. The vision is lifted, and Ezekiel tells the exiles everything. God tells Ezekiel, "The prince [ZEDEKIAH] will try to escape, but will not see Babylon." The false prophets are like jackals in Jerusalem, and the elders have idols in their heart. God sends four dreadful judgments to Jerusalem: sword, famine, wild beasts, and plague.

DAY 45

>─┼─◆>─O─<◆─┼─<

Ezekiel 15 to Ezekiel 24

Ezekiel continues to warn those left in Jerusalem. "God gave you gold and silver, but you made idols out of them. Like a prostitute, you were unfaithful, you will be judged like an unfaithful wife (spiritual adultery). Samaria was not half as bad as Jerusalem. Speak a parable about a great eagle. Babylon will capture Jerusalem. A righteous man, his son, and his son's son: a man will die for his own sins. God has no pleasure in the death of the wicked. Israel is like a lion captured and chained up. God brought you out of Egypt, but you rebelled. Therefore, the sword and terror. You despised the holy things. Aholah is Samaria, Aholibah is Jerusalem. You cast me—God—behind your back, and you will bear the sin of your idols."

DAY 46

Ezekiel 24 to Ezekiel 35

The king of Babylon lays siege to Jerusalem (the cooking pot), its filthiness is lewdness. You will not mourn when your sons and daughters are slain. The Ammonites are glad to see Israel in exile, therefore, God will destroy them. The same goes for the Philistines. Tyre will be scraped like a flat rock, and nations will mourn and lament. The king of Tyre will be cast down because of the pride and wickedness of his heart. The king of Egypt says he made the Nile River, so God will scatter Egypt for forty years. Egypt will be the wages for the army of Babylon. Egypt's allies will fall with her. Consider Assyria, once as beautiful as the garden of Eden, now cast out because of wickedness (take heed, Pharaoh). The watchman Ezekiel better blow the trumpet and warn the wicked man to turn to righteousness, and the righteous man not to become wicked! Woe to the shepherds (leaders) who rule the flock (people) with force and cruelty. "I, God, will place one shepherd from David's line, Jesus, who will be a prince over them, and I will be their God.
(Note: You have now read half the Bible.)

DAY 47

>━┥◆〉━O━〈◆┝━≺

Ezekiel 35 to Ezekiel 45

Prophesy against Mount Seir (Edom) because of the ancient hatred toward Israel: "You will be desolate, all of Idumea (Edom). Israel will come home (back to the land) and be better off than at the first. You (Israel) will be cleansed from your filthiness and idols. I (God) will put my spirit in you and you will loathe yourself for your sins. The land will be like the garden of Eden. The house of Israel is like dry bones, but they will become a great army. The two kingdoms will be united and become one. Gog and Magog will come against you (Israel) and bring many nations with them, a cloud of people. Israel will take seven months to bury the dead, and for seven years, they will use the weapons for fuel." Ezekiel has another vision fourteen years after Jerusalem is captured. A man, shining like bronze, measures the temple area, portico, gates, rooms, altar, and so on. A cubit is about eighteen inches, a long cubit is about twenty-one inches, and the reed is about ten and a half feet. The priests are to discern between the clean and unclean.

DAY 48

Ezekiel 45 to the end of Ezekiel; Hosea

Still in the vision, Ezekiel is told, "Give the Lord a holy portion of the land. Tell the prince to be fair with the people and make atonement for them. Keep the Passover, and when you enter the gate, exit by the opposite gate. A river flows from the temple with trees growing on both sides. The river gives life wherever it flows. Each tribe will have a portion of the land; the priests will have the holy portion. The city will have three gates on each side, twelve gates in all. The city will be called 'The Lord Is Here.'"

In the book of Hosea, his unfaithful wife represents how Israel, the northern kingdom, has been unfaithful to God; they have committed spiritual adultery. God says, "Turn from your adultery, or you will be stripped naked; you will lose everything and become worthless. Then in latter days, you will fear the Lord, but now there is no truth, mercy, or knowledge of God. You are proud and arrogant, but you will seek me in your affliction. I desire mercy, not sacrifice. This goes for Judah also. Your calf idol in Samaria will be broken and I will cast you away. It's time to seek the Lord, but you are bent on backsliding and sinning more and more! The righteous walk in my ways, but the rebellious stumble and fall."

DAY 49

>⊷⊶⊷O⊶⊷⊶<

Joel, Amos, Obadiah, and Jonah

People are told in Joel, "This has never happened before. Wake up, you drunkards! Sober up! Call for a fast, pray earnestly. The animals are suffering too. Sound the alarm. The day of the Lord is coming. A mighty army that the walls will not slow down. Weep, pray, and mourn. God will hear you and restore all things. He will pour out his spirit and show signs and wonders. The nations will be gathered against you and then judged. The sun, moon, and stars will be darkened. The fountain flows from the temple."

In Amos, they are told a shepherd has seen a vision in Israel about the nations around them. Jerusalem will be devoured by fire. Their bravest warriors will flee naked (without weapons). They will be led away with fish hooks. Only ten in every hundred will be left. But those who seek the Lord will live. Hate evil, love good. Burnt offerings will no longer be accepted as they turn justice into gall (poison). The end has come, but not totally, because The Lord will bring back the exiles.

There is another vision in Obadiah. Edom (Esau) will be destroyed because of the violence against Jacob (Israel, his twin brother).

In the book of Jonah, he is told to go to Nineveh (Assyria's capital) and warn them. But Jonah runs away and is tossed into the sea, where he is eaten by a large fish, who vomits him up. Nineveh repents, and Jonah is not happy because God is compassionate.

DAY 50

>—+◆>—O—<+—<

Micah, Nahum, Habakkuk,
and Zephaniah

In Micah, there is a vision of Samaria (northern kingdom) and Jerusalem (southern kingdom). Samaria will be a heap of rubble, and her sin reaches Jerusalem. Those who plot evil will be shaved bald when they go into exile. This place is defiled and ruined. Jerusalem's leaders accept bribes, so it will also become a heap of rubble. In the last days, many nations will stream to the temple to learn God's ways, but for now, they will go to Babylon. God brought them out of Egypt and showed them what is good. God will not be angry forever; he will show mercy.

Nahum presents a vision about Nineveh (Assyria). "You plot evil against the Lord, but the sword will devour you. Your army will become like women. Your wound will be a fatal injury."

Habakkuk asks, "Why does the Lord not listen to my cry for help? God says he is raising Babylon to sweep across the earth. Write the vision down, but woe to those who build cities with bloodshed. Calamity will come on them, and you, Israel, will rejoice in the Lord."

Zephaniah's vision is that "God will sweep both man and animals from the earth. The great day of the Lord is near. Gold and silver will not help you. Let the humble seek the Lord. Moab will become like Sodom and Gomorrah, a wasteland. Assyria will be desolate. All who call on the Lord will be purified."

DAY 51

>-·-‹•›-·-O-·-‹•›-·-<

Haggai, Zechariah, and Malachi

In Haggai, God tells them, "The people build their own houses, but not the house of the Lord. Now build the house of the Lord. When I shake the heavens and the earth, the nations will come and fill my house with silver and gold. From this day forward, I will bless you."

In the book of Zechariah, people are told to "Turn to me, God, and I will turn to you. Don't be like your forefathers." Zechariah, in a vision, sees a man on a red horse. Behind him are other horses who were sent across the earth. The temple and the cities will be rebuilt. Jerusalem will be rebuilt without walls; walls were for protection. "Many nations will become my people when the branch, Jesus, removes the sin in the land of Israel. Not by might or power, but by the Spirit. God's eyes search the whole earth. The flying scroll is the curse, and the woman in the basket is wickedness. The basket will be set in Shinar, (Babylonia)." Zechariah then sees the four chariots—the four spirits of heaven—in the vision. The people ask, "Should we continue to fast like we have for the past seventy years?" His answer is, "If you fast correctly, God will bless Jerusalem and Judah again. Your King will come riding a donkey. Take the thirty pieces of silver and throw it to the potter. Jerusalem will mourn and weep over the one they pierced. Strike the shepherd and scatter the sheep. The Lord will stand on the Mount of Olives, and it will be split from east to west. The Lord will be King over the whole earth, and every year, the nations will go to Jerusalem to worship him."

In Malachi, people are told, "The priests do not respect the Lord. They sacrifice a corrupt thing and cause many to stumble. Guard your spirit, and respect the wife of your youth. You rob God by not paying the tithe or giving offerings. Bring the tithe and be blessed. A book of remembrance was written for those who fear the Lord. Elijah will restore the hearts of the fathers and their children."

DAY 52

>–!–⟨•⟩–•–O–•–⟨•⟩–!–≺

Psalm 1 to Psalm 35

"The Lord watches over the righteous, but the wicked will perish. Kiss the Son. The Lord is a shield around me, so my sleep is peaceful. The Lord surrounds me with favor. Heal me and be merciful. You make the righteous secure. Children and infants praise the Lord. The Lord will never forsake those who seek him. He defends the fatherless. The eyes of the Lord watch over the righteous and give them protection. Sing to the Lord for he is good, a refuge to the poor. Walk blamelessly, dwell in his sanctuary, and you will not be shaken. God will hear and give ear to prayers. His ways are perfect. May my words and thoughts be pleasing to the Lord. I trust in God, not horses and chariots. God inhabits the praises of his people. I will dwell in the house of the Lord forever. The Lord is the King of Glory. Show me your ways, Lord. Examine my heart, and I will see your goodness. I will sing to you and give thanks. You bless your people with peace. Your favor lasts a lifetime. You deliver me from all my enemies and forgive the guilt of my sin. Your eyes are on those who fear you. Your angel encamps around those who fear you and he, the angel, delivers them."

DAY 53

>–⊱–⊱–✦–✧–⊰–⊰–✧

Psalm 35 to Psalm 67

"The wicked lay a snare for me without cause. They have no fear of God. Evil men will be cut off; they will be no more. O Lord, come quickly to my aid. A human life is but a breath; it is written in the scroll. Have mercy, and heal me for I have sinned against the Lord. My only hope is in the Lord, and I will praise him. Rescue me from deceitful and wicked men. I face death all day long, like sheep for the slaughter, yet you anoint me with the oil of joy. The Lord brings wars to an end and reigns over the nations. The kings of the earth are seized with pain, like a woman in labor. God will redeem my life. The wicked have no right to recite the Law (Torah). Create a pure heart in me, and grant me a willing spirit. Then I will flourish like an olive tree. A fool says there is no God. They attack me and seek my life. If I had wings like a dove, I would fly away. I trust in God, who delivers me from death. Great is your faithfulness and love. My enemies are like the venom of snakes. They turn on me like dogs, but God will trample them down. I will take refuge under God's wings and sing in his shadow. God protects me from my enemies and answers with awesome deeds. My enemies cringe before you, O Lord."

DAY 54

>━┼╍╾━O╍╾╌╾━┼━<

Psalm 67 to Psalm 91

"Let the people praise you, and then the land will yield its harvest. You are a father to the fatherless. Rescue me from the mire, the floodwaters, and the pit. Come quickly; you are my deliverer. My mouth will tell of your righteousness and salvation. You deliver those who cry out to you, but the arrogant are swept away suddenly. Remember your people, O God. You bring one down and exalt another. You alone are to be feared. I will meditate on your works and mighty deeds. You led your people out like a flock of sheep. Do not hold the sins of our forefathers against us. Restore us, and let your face shine on us. You rescue us in our distress. Rise up and judge the earth. Our enemies want to destroy us completely. One day in your courts is better than a thousand anywhere else. Your salvation is near. You are compassionate and gracious. Your foundation is on your holy mountain. I cry out to you in the morning. You have anointed your servant David with sacred oil. With you a thousand years are as one day."

DAY 55

⟐

Psalm 91 to Psalm 119

"When you rest in the shadow of the Almighty, he commands his angels to guard you. The righteous will flourish in the courts of our God. Holiness adorns your house, O Lord, and you know the thoughts of man. Do not harden your heart like those in the desert. The Lord comes to judge the earth, and the mountains will melt like wax. The Lord makes his salvation known for the Lord, our God, is holy. Enter his gates with thanksgiving and his courts with praise. No one who practices deceit or speaks falsely will stand in the house of the Lord. God responds to the destitute when they cry out. He removes our sins as far as the east is from the west. He is clothed in light, and he rides on the wings of the wind. He remembers his covenant with Abraham, Isaac, and Jacob, but our forefathers provoked him to anger with their wickedness. They cried out to him in their trouble, and he delivered them because of his great love. He stands at the right hand of the needy one. He will judge the nations. To fear the Lord is wisdom. Good things come to the generous person, but the wicked will be vexed. Praise the Lord now and forevermore. Tremble, O earth, in his presence. He is a help and shield to those who fear him. Call on the Lord for salvation for his love is great and endures forever."

DAY 56

>─┼─⟨⟩─O─⟨⟩─┼─≺

Psalm 119 to the end of Psalms

"I have hidden your word in my heart that I might not sin against you. You are a lamp to my feet. The Lord answers me in my distress and watches my coming and going. Pray for the peace of Jerusalem. Have mercy on us, Lord, for our help is in you. Like the mountains around Jerusalem, the Lord surrounds his people. Sow seeds in weeping and return with joy. Children are a reward from the Lord, and your wife is a fruitful vine. The Lord has cut the cords of the wicked, and with him is full redemption. Put your hope in the Lord. He has chosen Zion (Jerusalem). It is pleasant to live in unity. Lift your hands in the sanctuary. God makes the clouds and sends the rain. Give thanks to the Lord, his love endures forever. There is no joy in captivity. The Lord looks on the lowly and preserves his life. Search my heart, O God, is there any offensive way in me? The righteous will praise your name. Set a guard over my mouth and lips. Rescue me from those who pursue me. Answer me quickly. Train my hands for war and my fingers for battle. I will praise you every day. The Lord sustains the fatherless and the widow. He heals the brokenhearted. Praise the Lord for his splendor is above the earth and the heavens. Praise him with music and dancing. Let everyone who has breath praise the Lord."

DAY 57

Proverbs 1 to Proverbs 17

The fear of the Lord is the beginning of knowledge. Fools despise wisdom and discipline. Wisdom enters the heart, and knowledge is pleasant. Do not be wise in your own eyes. Do not walk in the path of the wicked and evil man. Man's ways are in full view of the Lord. Go to the ant, see its ways and be wise. Stay away from the adulteress, for her house is a highway to the grave. Find the Lord and find life and favor. If you try to correct a mocker or a wicked man, you are asking for trouble. A wise son gathers crops in the summer. A generous man prospers and people curse a selfish man. The way of the fool seems right to him, but a wise man seeks advice. Wickedness overtakes the sinner. There is a way that seems right to a man, but in the end, death. A gentle answer turns away wrath, and harsh words stir up anger. A perverse man stirs up dissension, and a gossip separates close friends.

DAY 58

>━┤◆>━○━<◆┤━<

Proverbs 17 to the end of Proverbs

An evil man is bent on rebellion. Life and death are in the tongue (your words). When you are kind to the poor, you are lending to the Lord. The Lord searches the spirit of a man and his inmost being. When you pursue righteousness and love, you will find life, prosperity, and honor. Thorns and snares are in the path of the wicked. Drunkards and gluttons become poor, so do not join them. Do not envy wicked men. It's better to live in a corner by yourself than to live with an unhappy wife. Without gossip, a quarrel dies down. Know the condition of your flocks and herds because riches are not forever. A stingy man is eager to get rich, but poverty awaits him. The righteous detest the dishonest, and the wicked detest the upright. Those who are pure in their eyes are never cleansed of their sin. The husband of an intelligent wife who fears the Lord is blessed with good and not evil. She is worthy of praise.

DAY 59

➤━◆➤━०━◆━◆

Job 1 to Job 22 (long O pronounced Jobe)

Job is a rich man with seven sons, three daughters, seven thousand sheep, three thousand camels, five hundred yoke of oxen, five hundred donkeys, and many servants. Satan tells God that the only reason Job serves him is because of the hedge of protection around him. In just one day, Satan destroys everything Job has, yet he sins not. Satan then afflicts Job with boils from head to toe. Job's friends Eliphaz, Bildad, and Zophar come and sit and weep with him for seven days without saying a word. Job says, "I wish I were never born. The thing I feared most has come upon me."

Eliphaz says, "If you plow evil and sow trouble, you will reap it. If I were you, I would appeal to God."

Job replies, "There is no wickedness on my lips."

Bildad says, "If you seek God and plead with him, he will restore you."

Job says, "I am blameless. Is there no one to umpire between me and God?"

Zophar asks, "Will your talk vindicate you? Should no one rebuke you when you mock? Put away your sin and evil."

Job answers, "I will argue my case with God. Your words are lies. Tell me my sin."

Eliphaz says, "Should a wise man talk like this? Your own mouth condemns you."

Job says, "You are miserable comforters. If you were in my place, I would speak words of encouragement and comfort. Now what hope do I have?"

"How long before you end your speeches? God has a place for the wicked," Bildad says.

Job says, "How long will you torment me? God has pulled me down with his net. My family and friends have left me. Have pity on me, my friends."

Zophar tells him, "The triumph of the wicked is short, and so is the hypocrites' joy. God will pour the fury of his wrath on him."

Job says, "Listen to me, then you can continue to mock me. How can you comfort me with your nonsense?"

DAY 60

>─┤◆>─◯─<◆├─<

Job 22 to the end of Job

Eliphaz explains to Job, "Your wickedness is great, and your sin is endless. Return to God, and he will restore you."

"I follow in his steps," says Job. "I keep his ways and follow his commandments and treasure his words."

Bildad asks, "How can a man be righteous before God?"

Job answers, "Who gave you these words? Can you understand God's power? I will not speak wickedness or deceit. I will never say you are right. I cry out to God, but he does not answer. He sees my ways and counts my steps."

After a brief silence, Elihu says, "I thought I was too young to speak, so I let you talk. Now listen to me. God repays man for what he has done, what his conduct deserves. His eyes are on his ways, his every step. The wicked man adds rebellion to his sin and multiplies his words against God. Now God is wooing you."

Then the Lord says to Job, "Brace yourself and answer me. Were you there when I created all this? The earth, the sea, the morning light, the lightning and the thunderstorm, the desert, the constellations, the lion, the mountain goats, the wild donkey, the wild ox, the ostrich, the horse, or the hawk? Answer me."

Job says, "I am unworthy. I will say no more."

The Lord says, "Would you condemn me to justify yourself? Consider the Behemoth. Can anyone capture him? Or Leviathan, can you tie him down? If you try once, you will never try again."

Job says, "You can do all things. I have heard of you, but now I see you."

God tells Job to pray for his three friends. He then blesses Job with twice as much as he had before.

DAY 61

Song of Songs, Ruth, and Lamentations

The Song of Solomon is a love song. "Your kisses are better than wine. Bring me into your chambers. I am the rose of Sharon, the lily of the valley. His banner over me is love. My beloved is mine, and I am his. How beautiful is your love? How delightful you are. Many waters cannot quench love."

Ruth is also a love story. Ruth stays with her mother-in-law after her husband dies. Ruth goes out to glean barley. When she brings a large amount home, Naomi finds out that Ruth was in the field of Boaz, a relative of Elimelech's. Boaz is a kinsman redeemer. Boaz marries Ruth, and she is the great-grandmother of King David.

In Lamentations, Jeremiah laments the destruction of Jerusalem. Judah is in exile. Pagans are in the sanctuary. No longer can Jerusalem keep her appointed feasts and Sabbaths. The false prophets fail to warn you of the captivity that will come. Young and old, men and women lie slain in the street. The Lord will not cast us off forever. We should examine our ways. Our punishment is worse than Sodom's. Our joy and dancing are gone because of our sins. Restore us, Lord. Renew our days of old.

DAY 62

>━┤◆╾━O━╼◆┝━<

Ecclesiastes, and Esther

In Ecclesiastes, King Solomon, the wisest man to ever live, searches for the meaning of life. "The sun rises and sets, only to rise again. There is nothing new. I chase the wind. I try pleasure, laughter, wine, folly, building, planting, irrigation, slaves, flocks and herds, silver and gold, a harem. I deny myself nothing, and I gain nothing. I must leave it all to someone who comes after me. I can only eat, drink, and enjoy my work. There is a time for everything, even death. God has set eternity in the heart of man, but can you even fathom it? Do you know if your spirit goes up or down? Did you make a vow to God? Fulfill it! The lover of money is never satisfied with his wealth. When you die, you go away naked. Try to leave a good name. A fool is quickly angered, and a live dog is better off than a dead lion. A little folly outweighs wisdom. Fear God, and keep his commandments for God will judge every deed, good or evil."

In the book of Esther, King Xerxes (Ahasuerus) has a banquet and sends for Queen Vasthi, who refuses to come. After consulting the wise men, the king banishes Queen Vasthi from his presence. After a search is made, the king finds a new queen, Esther, a Jew. Mordecai hears about a plot to kill the king and tells Queen Esther. Haman the Agagite hates Mordecai and all the Jews; he is unaware that Esther is a Jew. Haman makes a law that allows, on a certain day, anyone to kill as many Jews as he or she wants. Haman builds a gallows to hang Mordecai. Queen Esther makes the plot known to the king, and Haman is hanged on his own gallows. The law is overwritten—it could not be canceled—and the Jews have the upper hand. The Jews strike down their enemies with the sword for two days. The feast of Purim is celebrated to remember this victory.

DAY 63

><del>·|·<>·◦·<>·|·<del>

Daniel 1 to Daniel 10.

Daniel is taken captive by Nebuchadnezzar along with Shadrach, Meshach, and Abednego. These four men (boys, maybe teenagers or younger) would not eat the king's food, so God gives them knowledge, understanding, and wisdom. The king has a dream, and only Daniel can interpret it, and he is placed in a high position. Shadrach, Meshach, and Abednego are thrown into the furnace. Nebuchadnezzar is prideful, so God makes him eat grass with the wild animals. Belshazzar (Nebuchadnezzar's son) sees the handwriting on the wall and is slain that night. Darius the Mede (son of Xerxes, or Ahasuerus; remember Esther?) takes over the kingdom, and Daniel is thrown into the lions' den. Daniel has a dream (vision) about four beasts, and the fourth beast has ten horns. One of the horns wages war with the saints, but the court takes his power and gives it to the saints. Daniel has another vision, this one about a ram and a goat. The goat's horn is broken, and four other horns grow. One of the horns will stand against the prince, but he—the horn—will be defeated. The vision is about the end time. Daniel reads in Jeremiah about the seventy-year prophecy. Gabriel comes and interprets the vision. The abomination that causes desolation is set up in the temple.

DAY 64

Daniel 10 to the end of Daniel; Ezra 1 to Ezra 10

The vision concerns a great war between the king of the north and the king of the south. The man dressed in linen is helped by Michael because the prince of Persia fought for twenty-one days. The king of the south sends his daughter to the king of the north to make peace. It does not work. The king of the north sends his daughter to the king of the south to overthrow him. It does not work. The king of the north falls, and a contemptible person rises to power. The two kings meet face-to-face and lie to each other. The king of the north fights against the Holy Covenant and sets up the abomination that causes desolation. The king of the north comes to an end. The dead who sleep in the dust of the earth arise. The vision is sealed until the time of the end.

In Ezra, in the first year of Cyrus, the seventy years are complete, so he allows everyone who wants to return to Jerusalem and help rebuild the temple. He also returns all the articles taken from the temple of God. Almost fifty thousand people return to Judah and Benjamin. On the first day of the seventh month, they begin to offer burnt offerings to the Lord. The people give a great shout of praise when the foundation is finished. Their enemies living in the land send a letter to Artaxerxes, who forcibly stops the work. The prophets of God, Haggai and Zechariah, tell the people to work on the temple. Darius is now king, so another letter is sent to him. Darius searches the archives and orders the governor to pay the men their wages for working on the temple out of the royal treasury. The temple is completed in the sixth year of Darius. Ezra tells Artaxerxes that God will protect him and the people as they travel to Jerusalem. When he arrives, he finds out that the Jews have intermarried with foreign people.

127

DAY 65

>─┼─◆>─●─<◆┼─<

Ezra 10 to Nehemiah 11

Ezra calls for all the exiles to assemble in Jerusalem. He tells them to separate themselves from their foreign wives and children.

In Nehemiah, Artaxerxes gives Nehemiah permission to return to Jerusalem to rebuild the walls and gates. Sanballat and Tobiah mock him. Each family is given a section of wall and its gates to rebuild. Sanballat and Tobiah plan to kill them and put an end to the work. Nehemiah arms the people, and half are guards and half are workers; all wear a sword. The people complain about the high rate of interest being charged. Sanballat tries to lure Nehemiah away from the city to kill him. Tobiah has spies in the city to tell him everything Nehemiah says and does. Nehemiah reads the book of the Law (Torah) to the assembly, and they observe the feast of tabernacles (booths). That same month they renew the covenant and put their seal on it.

DAY 66

><+>+O+<+><

Nehemiah 11 to the end of Nehemiah; 1 Chronicles 1 to 1 Chronicles 6

The leaders live in Jerusalem, but the city needs more people. They cast lots for 10 percent of the people to live inside Jerusalem. The walls are dedicated with two choirs on top of the walls going in opposite directions and meeting in the temple. The sound of rejoicing is heard faraway. It is discovered that Tobiah has a room in the temple court. Nehemiah cleans house. A son of one of the high priests has married a daughter of Sanballat.

First Chronicles contains historical records starting from Adam. In chapter 4, the Simeonites (finally!) kill the remaining Amalekites when HEZEKIAH is king in Judah. The rights of the firstborn of Israel are given to Joseph's sons, Ephraim and Manasseh.

DAY 67

1 Chronicles 6 to 1 Chronicles 16

As king, David places some of the Levites as singers before the Tent of Meeting. Aaron's descendants present the burnt offerings. The Levites are given towns and pasturelands. Some of the Levites are gatekeepers stationed around the four sides of the Tent of Meeting. Other Levites are in charge of the flour, wine, oil, incense, spices, furnishings, and other articles. The musicians are exempt from other duties. When King Saul is killed in battle, the Philistines hang his head and armor in the temple of Dagon. David is made king over all Israel. He captures Jerusalem and calls it the "City of David" (Zion). The list of David's mighty men and their exploits includes Uriah the Hittite. Many of these men come to David when he is banished from Saul, and they become a great army. Uzzah dies when David puts the ark on a cart. The Levites carry the ark to Jerusalem, and David dances as they enter the city, and Michal (David's wife) despises him in her heart.

DAY 68

1 Chronicles 16 to 1 Chronicles 28

David appoints some Levites to minister regularly before the ark with the lyres, harps, cymbals, and trumpets. He also has the priests burn offerings and play music at the Tent of Meeting in Gibeon. David wants to build a house for the Lord, but God says his Son will build it. The Lord gives David victory everywhere he went. The gold, silver, and bronze are dedicated to the Lord. David sends a delegation to the Ammonites. The Ammonites and the Arameans wage war with Israel and are defeated. David tells Joab to count the fighting men in Israel. Seventy thousand men die from the plague. David buys the threshing floor and builds an altar. Then he says the temple will be built there. David informs Solomon that he will build the temple and then makes him king. The Levites' posts are appointed by casting lots. The army had twelve divisions, one for each month. There are twenty-four thousand men in each division. Joab is commander of the royal army.

DAY 69

1 Chronicles 28 to 2 Chronicles 12

David gives his personal treasury to the temple, and the officials and commanders also give willingly. Solomon is anointed king a second time. God appears to Solomon at Gibeon, at the Tent of Meeting. Solomon gets cedar logs from Hiram (king of Tyre). Hiram sends a skilled man to oversee the work. The threshing floor is where the temple is built. The inside is overlaid with gold; the doors are overlaid with bronze. All the bronze objects were cast in clay molds. The ark and the Tent of Meeting are brought to the temple. The musicians sang praises to the Lord, and the glory filled the temple. Solomon prays, and fire comes from heaven. The Lord appears to Solomon a second time. Solomon spends twenty years building the temple and his palace. The Queen of Sheba brings gold, spices, and gems to Jerusalem. The fleet of ships brought gold, silver, ivory, apes, and baboons. Solomon reigns for forty years, and then REHOBOAM becomes king, and the people revolt, splitting the kingdom. Judah and Benjamin are the only tribes to remain loyal. Many Levites leave the northern kingdom and join REHOBOAM.

(Note: You have read three quarters of the Bible.)

DAY 70

><+>+O+<+><

2 Chronicles 12 to 2 Chronicles 26

Egypt attacks Judah, and REHOBOAM repents. ABIJAH, the king of Judah, fights with Jeroboam (king of Israel) and defeats him. ASA destroyed the Cushite army and repairs the altar of the Lord. He then asks the king of Aram for help; he should have asked God. JEHOSHAPHAT joins with Ahab, the king of Israel, and goes to war against Aram. Ahab is killed. Ammon and Moab march against Judah, and God defeats them before JEHOSHAPHAT arrives. JEHORAM, JEHOSHAPHAT's son, kills his brothers and then dies a painful death. AHAZIAH teams up with the king of Israel and is killed. JOASH is made king when he is seven years old because his grandmother killed all his brothers. King JOASH has the temple repaired and then has Zachariah, the priest, stoned to death. JOASH is murdered. AMAZIAH defeats the Edomites and worships their idols. The king of Israel defeats AMAZIAH and breaks down a section of the walls of Jerusalem.

DAY 71

>─┼─◀▶─⊙─◀▶─┼─◅

2 Chronicles 26 to the end
of 2 Chronicles

UZZIAH becomes powerful by seeking the Lord. Because of pride, UZZIAH dies of leprosy. JOTHAM conquers the Ammonites and becomes powerful because he walks upright before God. AHAZ sacrifices his children in the fire. The Arameans defeat him and take many prisoners to Damascus. The king of Israel also defeats him, and the Philistines raid the towns. AHAZ closes the temple of God and sets up idol worship on every corner in Jerusalem. HEZEKIAH reopens the temple and invites all Israel (the northern kingdom) to the Passover (feast of unleavened bread). Then he cuts down the Asherah poles and smashes the sacred idol stones. God protects Jerusalem from the king of Assyria. HEZEKIAH becomes proud but then repents. MANASSEH sacrifices his sons in the fire and practices sorcery, divination, and witchcraft. The king of Assyria takes him prisoner. He then releases him and reopens the temple. AMON rejects God and worships idols, and then he is assassinated. JOSIAH turns to God and repairs the temple. The book of the Law is found, and Passover is observed. JOSIAH is killed in battle. Egypt carries JEHOAHAZ away and then places JEHOIAKIM on the throne. Nebuchadnezzar takes JEHOIAKIM to Babylon. JEHOIACHIN is also taken to Babylon. ZEDEKIAH will not listen to the prophets of God, so Jerusalem is burned, and the land has rest for seventy years.

DAY 72

>─┤◆├─○─┤◆├─<

Matthew 1 to Matthew 13

Matthew, Mark, Luke, and John each tell the account of Jesus as they remember. It is years after the resurrection when they write the gospels, so we have four views.

Matthew shares that Jesus is born in Bethlehem (in Judea) when Herod the Great was king. Herod kills all the boys two years old and under. John the Baptist is preaching, "Repent, for the kingdom of heaven is near." John baptizes Jesus. Satan tempts Jesus. Jesus leaves Nazareth and lives in Capernaum. Jesus begins preaching, calling his disciples, and healing the sick. Large crowds begin following him, so he sits down to teach them. The crowds are amazed because he teaches with authority. He heals the sick and drives out demons. The Pharisees claim he was driving out demons by the prince of demons. The apostles are Simon Peter, Andrew, James, John, Philip, Bartholomew, Thomas, Matthew, James, Thaddaeus, Simon, and Judas. John the Baptist sends his disciples to ask Jesus if he is the Christ. Jesus and his disciples are going through the grain fields when the Pharisees say they are breaking the Sabbath by picking grain. They are looking for a reason to accuse Jesus, so they could put him to death. The Scribes and Pharisees say, "Show us a sign!"

DAY 73

>-+-<>--O--<>-+-<

Matthew 13 to Matthew 24

The crowds are so large that Jesus gets into a boat to teach them. The disciples ask, "Why do you teach only parables?" Jesus replies, "The people's hearts are hard." Jesus could not do many miracles in Nazareth because of their lack of faith. Herod beheads John the Baptist. After Jesus feeds the five thousand families (men, women, and children) he walks on the water. The Pharisees accuse the disciples of breaking the Law (Torah). Jesus tells them, "Your worship is only rules taught by men." They were offended! After Jesus feeds four thousand families (men, women, and children), the Pharisees want to see a sign. Jesus warns the disciples to beware of the Pharisees' teaching. Jesus tells them that in Jerusalem, he would be killed and then raised on the third day. You must become like a child to enter the kingdom of God. The first will be last and the last first. Jesus rides into Jerusalem on a donkey, and the children praise him. The Pharisees were indignant! They ask about paying taxes. The Sadducees ask about the resurrection and then about the greatest commandment.

DAY 74

>━┼━◆➤━◯━◆┼━≺

Matthew 24 to Mark 6

The disciples ask Jesus about the end of the age. "The Son of Man will come on the clouds and send his angels with a loud trumpet. You don't know the day, so be ready. He will separate the sheep from the goats." The chief priests meet with Caiaphas, the high priest, and plot how to kill Jesus. In Bethany, a woman anoints Jesus for his burial. Judas gets thirty silver coins from the chief priests. The Lord's Supper is instituted, and Peter disowns Jesus. Judas returns the money and then hangs himself. Barabbas is released, and Jesus is crucified. After the Sabbath, the women go to the tomb and find it empty. The chief priests and elders give the guards money to say the disciples stole the body of Jesus.

The Gospel According to Mark tells how John the Baptist sees the spirit of God descend on Jesus. News about Jesus spreads quickly after he casts an evil spirit out of a man. Jesus can no longer enter a town openly after he heals a man of leprosy. After making a hole in the roof, four men lower a paralyzed man down to Jesus. The Pharisees are fasting and ask why the disciples are not fasting. The leaders start plotting how to kill Jesus after he heals a man on the Sabbath. The Scribes say that Jesus is possessed by Beelzebub. Jesus leaves in a boat, and then a violent storm hits. Jesus calms the storm, and the disciples are terrified, asking, "Who is this that even the wind and waves obey him?" As Jesus goes to the house of Jairus, a synagogue ruler, a woman touches his clothes and is healed.

DAY 75

>→I◆→-O-←◆I-◄

Mark 6 to the end of Mark

Jesus sends the twelve disciples out two by two. When Herod hears about Jesus, he says, "John the Baptist has been raised from the dead." The Pharisees ask why the disciples eat with unwashed hands and again ask for a sign. After the transfiguration, Jesus tells Peter, James, and John not to tell anyone about it. James and John ask for the seat on the right and left hands of Jesus. After Jesus rides into Jerusalem on a colt, he overturns the moneychangers' tables. The chief priests ask Jesus where he gets his authority. Jesus says, "The teachers of the law devour widows' houses. Nation will rise against nation, there will be earthquakes and famines, you will be arrested and hated, children will revolt, and the Lord will cut those days short." Jesus then says, "One of the twelve will betray me, and you will all fall away." Jesus is arrested, and the Sanhedrin hands him over to Pilate. Simon from Cyrene is forced to carry the cross. After the Sabbath, the women are told, "Tell the disciples that Jesus has risen."

DAY 76

>⊶⊶⊙⊶⊷≺

Luke 1 to Luke 9

Luke investigates before he writes his book. During the time of Herod the Great, the angel Gabriel is sent to the priest Zachariah, John the Baptist's father, and to Mary, the mother of Jesus. Gabriel tells Mary that Jesus will reign over the house of Jacob forever. Caesar Augustus, the Roman emperor, wants the people numbered, so Joseph and Mary go to Bethlehem, where Jesus is born. When Jesus is twelve years old, his parents find him in the temple, talking to the teachers of the Law. John the Baptist starts preaching when Tiberius Caesar is emperor. (Herod and Philip are the sons of Herod the Great.) Herod puts John in prison as it was not legal for Herod to have Philip's wife. After Jesus is baptized, he returns to Nazareth, and the people reject him. He moves to Capernaum, where he heals the sick and casts out demons. Jesus tells Peter to let his net down for a catch of fish, and they fill two boats (Peter, James, and John are partners). Jesus eats with tax collectors and sinners. All the people want to touch him as the power is coming from him. Jesus says, "Be kind to your enemies because God is kind to the ungrateful and wicked. You will know a tree (man) by his fruit (deeds)." In Nain, Jesus raises a dead man. The seed is the word of God, and all are included in this parable (the path, rocks, thorns, and good soil). Jesus raises a girl from the dead.

DAY 77

>──┤─◆>──O──<◆─┤──<

Luke 9 to Luke 17

Jesus says, "Deny yourself, and take up your cross daily." A voice from the cloud tells Peter, James, and John, "This is my son, listen to him." The disciples argue about who is the greatest among them. Jesus sends them out like lambs among wolves. Jesus says, "If (or when) they reject you, they reject me." Jesus and his disciples eat at the home of Mary and Martha. The disciples say, "Teach us to pray." Jesus tells them, "Ask, seek, and knock." He also says, "If an evil spirit returns to a man, it returns with seven other evil spirits. If your eyes are good, your whole body is full of light. Woe to the lawyers (teachers) who take away the key of knowledge. Beware of greed; your life is more than just what you have, so seek the kingdom of God. A family of five will be divided two against three. Enter through the narrow gate. Be sure to invite the poor, crippled, lame, and blind, and then you will be blessed. Salt is no good if it loses its saltiness. There is rejoicing in the presence of the angels over one sinner who repents. If you are dishonest a little bit, you cannot—will not—be trusted with much."

DAY 78

>─┼─⟡─┼─O─┼─⟡─┼─<

Luke 17 to the end of Luke

Jesus heals ten lepers, and only one, a Samaritan, returns to thank him. Will the Son of man find faith on the earth? Humble yourself, and God will exalt you. What is impossible with men is possible with God. Outside Jericho, Jesus heals a blind man. Inside Jericho, Jesus greets Zacchaeus. The stone the builders rejected has become the cornerstone. God is the God of the living, not the dead. The poor widow puts all she has in the treasury. Satan asks to sift Simon (Peter) like wheat, but Jesus prays for him. Judas leads a crowd to the Mount of Olives, where they arrest Jesus. Peter cuts a man's ear off, and Jesus puts it back on. Jesus looks straight at Peter when the rooster crows. Pilate sends Jesus to Herod, and Herod sends him back to Pilate. Herod and Pilate become friends. Jesus is crucified between two criminals. Joseph from Arimathea places Jesus's body in a new tomb. After the resurrection, Jesus talks with two people on the road to Emmaus. He opens their minds so they can understand the scriptures.

DAY 79

John 1 to John 9

John, who wrote this book, is not John the Baptist. In the beginning the word (Jesus) was with God when they, together, create everything, and the word (Jesus) becomes flesh (man). John the Baptist is the voice in the wilderness to prepare the way for Jesus, who will baptize you with the Holy Spirit. The Law comes through Moses, but truth and grace come through Jesus. Jesus says, "Destroy this temple, and I will raise it in three days. No one can enter the kingdom unless he is born of water and the spirit. Moses lifted up the snake in the wilderness, so also the Son of Man must be lifted up. Whoever believes is not condemned, whoever does not believe is condemned. Everyone who does evil hates the light. Whoever believes in the Son has eternal life. True worshippers worship the Father in spirit and truth. The fields are ripe for harvest." Jesus heals a man and says, "Stop sinning, or something worse may happen to you," and, "I only do what the Father tells me." A boy gives his lunch (five loaves and two fish) to Jesus. Jesus then feeds five thousand families (men, women, and children) and has twelve baskets of leftovers. Jesus is the bread of life, and no one comes to him unless the Father draws him (the bread is his flesh). His words are spirit and life. At the feast of tabernacles, Jesus says, "Streams of living water will flow from within him who believes. Everyone who sins is a slave to sin. If the Son sets you free you will indeed be free. The devil is a liar and the father of lies. Before Abraham was, I Am."

DAY 80

John 9 to John 18

Jesus tells his disciples, "Do the work of God while it is day; night is coming." The Jews expel the man born blind from the synagogue. Jesus says, "The good shepherd lays down his life for the sheep (humankind). My sheep (followers) know my voice." Jesus raises Lazarus from the dead. Mary, the sister of Lazarus, pours perfume on Jesus. Jesus rides into Jerusalem on a donkey. Jesus says, "The prince of the world (Satan) will be driven out. I have come into the world as a light." At the Last Supper, Jesus washes the disciples' feet. Judas leaves as soon as Jesus gives him a piece of bread. Jesus says, "All men will know you are my disciples by the love you show. I go to prepare a place for you. You will do greater things than I have done when the comforter (Holy Spirit) has come. I give you my peace, do not be afraid. If you obey my commandments, you will remain in my love. Anyone who hates me hates the Father (God). They will kill you thinking they are doing the work of God. The spirit of truth will guide you. Father, protect them from the evil one."

DAY 81

John 18 to Acts 8

After Peter cuts Malchus's ear off, the detachment of soldiers bind Jesus and take him to Annas for questioning. Annas sends him to Caiaphas, and they send him to Pilate. Pilate has him flogged, and they put a crown of thorns on his head. The chief priests and officials shout, "Crucify him!" Pilate hangs a sign on the cross: "Jesus of Nazareth, King of the Jews." When one of the soldiers pierces Jesus's side, blood and water gush out. Joseph and Nicodemus place Jesus in the tomb. Mary Magdalene runs to Peter and another disciple, John, and tells them Jesus is missing. Mary sees Jesus in the garden. Thomas is the last of the disciples to see Jesus. Peter, Thomas, Nathanael, James, John, and two other disciples go fishing and see Jesus. Jesus tells Peter, "Follow me."

The book of Acts was written by Luke. In his version, Jesus tells the disciples to wait in Jerusalem until they receive the Holy Spirit. Jesus ascends into heaven while they watch. Matthias takes Judas's place as a disciple. When they are filled with the Holy Spirit, the crowd says they are drunk. Peter says, "Repent and be baptized," and three thousand are added to their number. Peter and John heal a crippled man, so the Jewish leaders arrest them. The believers start sharing their wealth with those in need. Ananias and Sapphira lie to the Holy Spirit and fall over dead. The sick people are brought to Jerusalem, and all are healed. The Jewish leaders arrest the disciples, and an angel sets them free. They arrest them again and have them flogged and warn them, "Do not speak about Jesus." But they keep on preaching. A large number of priests become believers. Stephen is falsely accused and brought before the Sanhedrin. He is stoned to death while Saul watches.

DAY 82

>━┼━◆>━━O━━<◆━┼━<

Acts 8 to Acts 18

Saul begins arresting the believers, and all but the disciples (apostles) are scattered; they all leave Jerusalem. Simon the Sorcerer offers Peter and John money. Philip baptizes the Ethiopian. Saul becomes a believer and starts preaching the gospel. Peter preaches in the house of Cornelius (a Gentile), and the Holy Spirit comes on all in the house. The apostles say, "Wow! Even the Gentiles can receive." Barnabas and Saul go to Antioch, where the believers are called "Christians." After King Herod kills James, he arrests Peter. An angel sets him free, so Herod has the prison guards executed. On the island of Cyprus, Saul is called Paul. John Mark returns to Jerusalem. The Jews turn against Paul and Barnabas, so they preach to the Gentiles. In Lystra, the crowds call Paul "Hermes" and Barnabas "Zeus" (gods). Paul is stoned to death—they think. Some men from Judea tell the Gentiles they must be circumcised and follow the Laws of Moses. The elders, by the Holy Spirit, decide the only requirements for Gentile believers it that they abstain from, "food sacrificed to idols, blood, meat from strangled animals, and sexual immorality." Paul travels with Silas, and Barnabas travels with John Mark. Paul meets Timothy. A riot starts when Paul casts a demon out of a slave girl. The Jews continue to oppose Paul and the gospel.

DAY 83

>––‹›–⦾–‹›–⦿

Acts 18 to the end of Acts

In Corinth, the Lord tells Paul, "Fear not, speak the word, do not be silent." Paul shaves his head because of a vow. Some handkerchiefs and aprons that Paul touches are taken to the sick, and they recover. Some Jews (seven priests) try to invoke the name of Jesus to cast demons out, but the demons drive them out. A silversmith starts a riot in Ephesus because of the gospel. Paul preaches so long that a young man falls from a third-floor window and is killed. Paul raises him from the dead and then continues to talk until daylight. Paul says he is going to Jerusalem, and they will never see him again. A prophet tells Paul the Jews in Jerusalem will bind him and hand him over to the Gentiles. In Jerusalem, the Roman commander stops the crowd from killing Paul. The Lord tells Paul that he will stand before Caesar. The Jews plot to kill Paul, so the commander sends Paul to Felix, the governor. After two years, Festus is governor, and Paul asks to stand before Caesar. As Paul is being taken to Rome, the ship is destroyed but no lives are lost. Paul is bitten by a deadly snake. In Rome, Paul is allowed to rent a place with a Roman guard for two years.

DAY 84

>━┥━◆〉━●━〈◆━┥━<

Romans 1 to the end of Romans

Paul is writing to the Gentile believers in Rome about God's grace and judgment. The Law (Torah) does not make us righteous; it is faith in Jesus, both Jews and Gentiles. Abraham is justified by faith, and we are also justified by faith. Sin and death enter the world through one man, Adam, and through one man, Jesus, enter grace and righteousness. You were once slaves to sin, but now slaves to righteousness. Sin brings death, but God's gift is eternal life through Jesus Christ. Those controlled by the sinful nature cannot please God. We who are controlled by the Spirit of God are children of God. God works for the good of those who love him. Confess with your mouth that Jesus is Lord, and believe in your heart that God raised him from the dead, and you will be saved. Salvation has come to the Gentiles to make the Jews envious. Hate what is evil; love what is good. Try to live at peace with everyone. Love is the fulfillment of the Law (Torah). The kingdom of God is righteousness, peace, and joy in the Holy Spirit. Beware of those who cause division.

DAY 85

1 Corinthians

The church at Corinth has many questions that Paul answers in this letter. The cross is foolishness to those perishing, but to the saved, it is the power of God. To the natural man, it is spiritually discerned. Everyone's work will be tested by fire. The Lord will expose the hidden things of darkness. There is even sexual sin in the church. The unrighteous will not inherit the kingdom of God. There is one God, the Father, and one Lord, Jesus. Exercise self-control as you run the race of life. Israel's history is an example of what happens when you set your heart on evil desires. All temptation is common to man. Flee from idolatry. When you take the Lord's Supper, you proclaim his death. There are many gifts given by the Holy Spirit for everyone's benefit. Desire the best gifts. If you don't have love, you are just a lot of noise. You have faith, hope, and love, and love is the greatest. Desire the gift of prophecy. Don't forget that Christ died for your sins, was buried, and was raised on the third day. He is the first fruits of those who have died. When the last trumpet sounds, the dead will be raised. Take your stand, and be firm in the faith.

DAY 86

>-I-◆>-←O-←◆>-I-≺

2 Corinthians; Galatians

God comforts us in our troubles so that we can comfort others in their troubles. We spread the fragrance of Christ everywhere we go. When Moses is read, a veil covers their hearts until they turn to the Lord. The god of this age has blinded the minds of unbelievers until they see the light. Fix your eyes on what is unseen, eternal, not on what is seen, temporary. When you are at home in the body, you are absent from the Lord. We must all appear before the judgment seat of Christ. We are a new creation in Christ. Now is the day of salvation. Touch no unclean thing, and purify yourself. Godly sorrow brings repentance unto salvation. When you give generously, you reap generously; this is your expression of thanks to God. The weapons we use have divine power to take down strongholds, demons. When you boast, boast in the Lord. Satan himself appears as an angel of light, so beware of his servants. A messenger of Satan is a thorn in Paul's flesh to keep him from boasting. Paul says, "I am writing this to you now, so I will not have to be harsh with you when I come."

Galatians remarks on how quickly you have turned away from the gospel! Some false brothers have come in to compel you to be circumcised (follow the Law). We know that a man is not justified by observing the Law (Torah) but by faith in Jesus Christ. The righteous will live by faith, not the Law. Stand firm, and do not become burdened. The law is summed up in a single command, "Love your neighbor as yourself." Those who belong to Christ have crucified the sinful nature. Do not become weary in doing good.

DAY 87

>━┤◆>━O━<◆┤━<

Ephesians, Philippians, Colossians, and 1 Thessalonians

In Ephesians, Paul hopes that God gives you the spirit of wisdom and knowledge so you may know Jesus better. You have been saved by grace through faith so that Jews and Gentiles will become one, Christ being the cornerstone. This is the mystery of the gospel. You must no longer live as the Gentiles. Do not grieve the Holy Spirit. Put off bitterness, rage, anger, brawling, slander, malice, sexual immorality, impurity, greed, obscenity, foolish talk, and coarse joking. Live as children of the light, and find out what pleases the Lord. Sing and make music in your heart to the Lord. Our struggle is against the spiritual forces of evil. You need the armor of God to stand your ground.

Paul tells us in Philippians that all the palace guard knows he is in chains for Christ. To live is Christ, and to die is gain. Every knee will bow, and every tongue will confess Jesus is Lord. Work out your salvation with fear and trembling. Forget what is behind, and press forward. The cross has many enemies. Think about the things that are true, noble, right, pure, lovely, admirable, excellent, and praiseworthy.

In Colossians, Christ has rescued you from darkness. Do not let anyone take you captive through false doctrine. Do not worship angels. Clothe yourself with compassion, kindness, humility, gentleness, and patience. Anyone who does wrong will be repaid for his wrong. Devote yourself to prayer.

In 1 Thessalonians, you receive our words as they were straight from God. The Jews try to keep us from sharing with the Gentiles, but you are standing firm in the Lord. Be sanctified, and avoid sexual immorality. At the last trumpet call, the dead will rise and meet in the air those who are still alive. Sudden destruction will come when people proclaim, "Peace! Peace!" Do not pay back wrong for wrong. Hold on to the good, and avoid the evil.

DAY 88

>··│··◇··○··◇··│··<

2 Thessalonians; 1 and 2 Timothy; Titus; and Philemon

In 2 Thessalonians, the Lord will be revealed in blazing fire with powerful angels, but first the rebellion occurs. The man of sin will oppose God and deceive those who perish. Therefore, stand firm in the Lord Jesus Christ. Warn the brothers—fellow believers—who are idle. If a man won't work, neither shall he eat.

In 1 Timothy, Paul warns that there are those who want to be teachers, but they teach false doctrine. Fight the good fight, and hold on to the faith. Pray for those in authority. God wants all men to be saved. In latter times, some will turn away from the faith. The sins of some men are obvious; others are revealed later. Those who teach false doctrine stir up controversies and quarrel about words. Turn away from opposing ideas that are falsely called knowledge.

In 2 Timothy, stir up the gift of God that you have. Everyone who confesses the name of Jesus must turn from wickedness. Those who quarrel have been trapped by the devil. In the last days, people will have a form of godliness but deny its power. Evil men and imposters will get worse and worse, deceiving many and turn from the truth.

In Titus, I left you in charge to appoint elders in the church. Pay no attention to Jewish myths. Say no to ungodliness and evil desires. We are saved because of God's mercy. Warn a divisive person.

Paul says in Philemon that your runaway slave has become a believer, so he asks you to welcome him back as a brother.

DAY 89

>–I–‹›–O–‹›–I–‹

Hebrews, author unknown

In the past, God talked through the prophets, but now he speaks through his Son. You will not escape if you ignore this great salvation. Jesus now calls us brothers, and because he was tempted, he knows how to help those who are tempted. Do not harden your heart by sin's deceitfulness. You must combine the message with faith. God's Word judges the thoughts and attitudes of the heart. Jesus has become our high priest. A change in the priesthood also brings a change in the Law (Torah). God found fault with the people, so a new covenant is needed. The old covenant is obsolete, with its regulations for worship using the blood of goats and bulls. Now Jesus offers his own blood because without the shedding of blood, there is no forgiveness of sin. Once Jesus offered his blood, he sat down at the right hand of God, so the old sacrifices will no longer be accepted. By faith you know that God created the universe, so by faith, we fix our eyes on Jesus. Live at peace with everyone and be holy. The kingdom of God cannot be shaken. Be sure to entertain strangers; they might be angels. The sacrifices you offer from now on are praise to Jesus with our lips. Do this continually.

DAY 90

><i<>·O·<>i<

James; 1 and 2 Peter; 1, 2, and 3 John

The book of James tells us that if you lack wisdom, ask God. Take care of the widows and orphans; it's part of your faith. Watch your tongue. Resist the devil. Do not judge. The Lord's coming is near.

1 Peter says that you are redeemed by the precious blood of Jesus Christ. Resist sinful desires that war against your soul. You are like sheep gone astray. Treat your wife with respect. The end of all things is near. The devil wants to devour you. Resist him.

In 2 Peter, make sure you keep reminding yourself of these things. Don't be like a pig that has been washed and then returns to the mud. Beware of scoffers who ask, "Where is this coming?" The Lord's coming will bring destruction by fire, and then a new heaven and new earth. Grow in the grace and knowledge of Jesus Christ.

1 John says that God is light with no darkness. If you hate a brother, darkness has blinded you. The Antichrist denies the Father and the Son. Everyone born of God no longer lives in sin. Those who obey his commands live in him, and he lives in us. God is love. Perfect love casts out fear. The one who has the Son has eternal life.

In 2 John, to walk in obedience to his commands is to love one another. Beware of deceivers.

3 John warns that anyone who does evil is not from God.

DAY 91

>━┥◆>━◯━<◆┥━<

Jude; Revelation 1 to Revelation 12

Jude warns that Godless men turn the grace of God into a license for immorality. In the last days, scoffers will come and divide you. Have mercy on those who doubt.

The book of Revelation is the revelation of Jesus Christ to John the apostle, imprisoned on the island of Patmos for preaching the gospel. Jesus says, "Write to the 7 churches," and, "I hold the keys of death and Hades." His voice is like a trumpet. John stands before the throne in heaven. The twenty-four elders lay their crowns before the throne. The Lamb is the only one worthy of opening the scroll. The scroll has seven seals. When the sixth seal is opened, there is a great earthquake. A seal is placed on the foreheads of 144,000 from Israel. A great multitude from every nation, tribe, people, and language are before the throne wearing white robes of righteousness. After the seventh seal, seven angels prepare to sound seven trumpets. After the sixth trumpet, the beast will kill the two witnesses, but after three and a half days, they will rise from the dead. After the seventh trumpet, God's temple in heaven is opened, and the Ark of the Covenant is seen.

DAY 92

>─┼─♦>──O──<♦─┼─<

Revelation 12 to the end of Revelation

Woe to those on earth because the devil, Satan, has been hurled to the earth with his angels. All the people on the earth will worship the beast unless their name is written in the Book of Life. Anyone who receives the mark of the beast will drink of God's fury. Seven angels are given seven bowls (one each) filled with God's wrath (the seven plagues). When the seventh bowl is poured out, it's the worst earthquake ever. The kings of the earth commit adultery with the great prostitute. Babylon the great falls in one hour. Rejoice and be glad because the wedding of the Lamb has come. The beast and the false prophet are thrown into the fiery lake. Satan is bound for a thousand years. The dead, both great and small, stand before the great white throne, and the books are opened. The first heaven and the first earth pass away. A new heaven and new earth are formed, and the new Jerusalem comes down from heaven! God will dwell among the people. Jesus says, "Behold, I am coming soon. Blessed are those who wash their robes. Yes, I am coming soon."

EPILOGUE

You should read the Bible every day, and read it all the way through at least once every year. After reading it through a few times, you will start putting the family names together. Some of the names are hard to pronounce, but remember, they are not American names. The Hebrew Scriptures were translated into Greek under the Roman Empire. Much of the Hebrew Scriptures are no longer available, so the Greek and Latin translations are where we get our modern translations. For more information, research the "Dead Sea Scrolls". The New Testament was written in Greek. Therefore, all translations are a translation. Ask God, and he will give you insight because the Word is alive and relevant for today.

Printed in the United States
By Bookmasters